The Signs Animals Leave

The Signs Animals Leave

Frank Staub

Watts LIBRARY

Franklin Watts
A Division of Scholastic Inc.
New York • Toronto • London • Auckland • Sydney
Mexico City • New Delhi • Hong Kong
Danbury, Connecticut

*For Prairie, Sasha, and Springs,
who left permanent signs in my heart.*

Note to readers: Definitions for words in **bold** can be found in the Glossary at the back of this book.

All Photographs ©: Frank J. Staub.
Author's photo by Marsha Kinkade.

The photograph on the cover shows a spider's web. The photograph opposite the title page shows tracks left in the sand by a great blue heron.

Library of Congress Cataloging-in-Publication Data

Staub, Frank J.
　　The signs animals leave / Frank Staub.
　　　　p. cm.— (Watts Library)
　　Includes bibliographical references and index.
　　ISBN 0-531-11863-0 (lib. bdg.)　　0-531-16575-2 (pbk.)
　　1. Animal tracks—Juvenile literature. 2. Animal tracks. 3. Animals—Habits and behavior. I. Title. II. Series.
QL768 .S737 2001
590—dc21　　　　　　　　　　　　　　　　　　　　　　　　　　　　　　00-043603
　　　　　　　　　　　　　　　　　　　　　　　　　　　　　　　　　　　　　CIP

© 2001 Franklin Watts, a Division of Scholastic Inc.
All rights reserved. Published simultaneously in Canada.
Printed in the United States of America.
1 2 3 4 5 6 7 8 9 10 R 10 09 08 07 06 05 04 03 02 01

Contents

Chapter One
Animal Stories 7

Chapter Two
On the Trail 11

Chapter Three
Dropped Signs 21

Chapter Four
Among the Trees 27

Chapter Five
In the Open 37

Chapter Six
Along the Shore 47

52 **Glossary**

56 **To Find Out More**

59 **A Note on Sources**

61 **Index**

A row of tiny tracks, a hole in the snow, and the scrape marks of flapping wings tell the story of how a mouse met its end.

Chapter One

Animal Stories

The night air is still. Fresh snow covers the land. A mouse leaves its hiding place and scampers across a meadow. In a nearby tree, a hungry owl takes notice. Silently, it swoops down. As the big bird pounces, it pushes its tiny meal into the snow, scraping the surface with its wings.

The next morning, a skier glides past the spot where the owl and mouse met. She pauses, and sees a row of tiny footprints ending in a hole. Lines have been scraped around the hole. Looking at the marks in the snow, she can read the story of last night's drama even though she was not there to see it. Animal **signs** can provide a lot of information about life in the natural world.

The World of Animal Signs

The world is full of animal signs such as those that told the story of the owl and the mouse. **Tracks**, or footprints, are the most common signs. Animals also leave **scat**, or droppings of body waste. In addition, many animals may make some kind of nest, scraping, rubbing, mound, dam, hole, tunnel or chew mark that people can use to learn about their behavior.

Sometimes, animals leave signs on other animals. An alligator's missing foot may have been bitten off by another alligator. A large wound on a sea lion's back was probably made by a shark. Sharp quills in the face of a bison, or American buffalo, were left there by a porcupine hidden in the grass.

People hardly ever see most wild animals. Some come out only late at night. Others might be nervous around people, and are too shy to show themselves when humans are nearby. Tracks and other signs are often the only way we know that these animals are around. That's why many people who study, work, or live around wild animals learn how to read their signs.

Reading signs was one of the skills our ancestors used while hunting for food. Today, scientists studying rare animals get much of their information from signs. By learning to read animal signs, you may be able to answer questions such as:

> **Another Name for Signs**
>
> Tracks and other signs are sometimes called an animal's **spoor**. The term comes from a Dutch word for track.

- What **species** or kind of animal made a sign?
- What does that animal eat?
- Was it alone?
- How fast was it moving?
- How long ago did it pass this way?

Trying to answer questions such as these isn't always easy, but it can be exciting.

How do you think this bison got a face full of porcupine quills?

A beetle makes tracks in the sand.

Chapter Two

On the Trail

Most animal tracks are just depressions in the ground. Clear tracks that show all the details of an animal's foot are rare. You may be able to find a good track if you follow the animal's **trail**, a line of tracks or other signs. When you follow an animal's trail, you are **tracking**. Never step on the tracks while tracking. You may want to come back later for a closer look.

A trail may lead you to the animal itself. If it does, keep your distance. A wild animal has a hard life. Don't make it harder by disturbing it. Also, any creature may become dangerous if it gets

Cats Versus Dogs

Both cats and dogs have four toes per foot, but you can still tell cat tracks from dog tracks. Canine prints are longer than they are wide, and often show claw marks. Feline tracks have no claw marks, because cats can pull in their claws. A feline track may appear round. The main pad of a feline foot bulges forward in two places behind the toes. The main pad of a dog's foot has just one bulge.

scared. If you can watch a wild animal from a safe distance, wait until it leaves. Then take a close look at the spot where it was. This is a great way to see the signs it left.

Toe Walkers

The heels of many animals don't show in their tracks. This is true for **feline** animals, members of the cat family such as lynx, mountain lions, and bobcats. It's also true for **canines**, members of the dog family such as wolves, foxes, and coyotes. Only humans, bears, and certain small creatures have heels that touch the ground.

The footprints of canines, felines, and many other animals are made by **pads** on the bottoms of their feet. These soft, thick areas absorb shock and keep the feet from slipping around. The largest pad covers the area that in humans is called the ball of the foot. These animals have smaller pads on their toes.

Ungulates don't show heel marks either. Ungulates are plant-eating animals such as deer, cows, and horses that usually have **hooves** protecting their toes. A hoof is a hard

Deer tracks are often difficult to tell apart from those of other cloven-footed animals. Sometimes deer tracks are heart-shaped and sometimes each half of the track may be separated. This animal was moving from left to right.

bony covering on the toe. Animal hooves are made of the same substance as your fingernails. Sheep, goats, antelope, javelinas (a relative of pigs), and members of the deer family such as moose, elk, and deer are ungulates with **cloven feet**. The hoof of a cloven-footed ungulate consists of two parts. Each part is a modified toe. In contrast, horses, donkeys, and zebras do not have cloven feet. These ungulates walk on just one toe. With such simple feet, ungulates can run quickly. Ungulates must run to stay alive, because they are a favorite food of canine and feline hunters.

Some animal species with fewer than five toes on a foot have **dewclaws**. Dewclaws are small toes that serve no practical purpose. They are higher on the leg than the toes on the feet. Canines and felines have one dewclaw on each leg. Members of the deer family have two. When deer walk in snow or soft mud, dewclaw marks may show in their tracks.

> **Use Your Nose**
>
> If a line of tracks detours next to an object such as a tree or rock, smell the object. If it smells like a cat's litter box, you may be on the trail of a bobcat or mountain lion.

Searching for Clues

To read animal signs, you have to be like a detective searching for clues. To solve the mystery, it helps to know what kinds of animals live in the area and what kind of **habitats** those animals like best. An animal's habitat is the kind of place where the animal normally lives. You won't find a mountain goat track at the beach, or a sea otter track in the desert.

If you find a good track, its shape will tell you the **family** of the animal that made it. A family is a group of different species with similar characteristics. For example, in the deer family, moose, elk, and deer all have heart-shaped tracks. Once you know the family, the track's size may tell you the species. Track size usually varies with body size. Moose are larger than elk, and elk are larger than deer. Likewise, moose tracks are larger than elk tracks, and elk tracks are larger than deer tracks. However, this trick doesn't always work. A young elk may have tracks that are the same size as those of an adult deer.

The season when a track was made may also help pin down what animal made it. For example, ground squirrel prints and tree squirrel prints are similar. Both animals have four toes on their front feet and five toes on their larger hind feet. However, squirrel tracks on the snow are probably those of a tree squirrel, because ground squirrels **hibernate**, or sleep most of the winter.

Seeing where a trail ends is another important clue to an animal's identity. Tree squirrel trails often lead from one tree to another. Ground squirrel trails end at a hole in the ground where the animal lives.

How Fast Did It Go?

The front feet of cats, dogs, and ungulates are larger than their hind feet. Mice, bears, rabbits, squirrels, weasels, raccoons, and opossums have larger hind feet. The track pattern of a walking animal shows each hind foot on top of or very close to the front track on the same side. If the animal speeds up, its hind feet may land in front of its front prints. As it goes faster and faster, its rear prints appear farther and farther forward.

A bird hopping across the sand of a dry stream left a paired track pattern.

Experienced trackers often depend on the pattern of tracks as much as the tracks themselves. **Track pattern** is the position of the tracks in relation to each other. For example, tree squirrels usually hop with both front feet together when they are on the ground. That's why the front tracks of tree squirrels are **paired**, or side by side. In contrast, ground squirrels walk by putting one foot forward and then the other. This gives ground squirrels an **alternate** track pattern. Their front tracks are not side by side.

Becoming a Tracker

As you look at tracks, you will find that tracks in some surfaces are easier to study than tracks in others. Tracks in soil that contains lots of clay keep their sharp edges the longest. Tracks in sand fade quickly, especially in the wind. Mud that isn't too wet, and fresh, slightly moist snow are two of the best surfaces for studying tracks and the patterns they form. When tracking on the snow, pay special attention to tracks in shady areas. Here the tracks appear sharper because the sun hasn't had a chance to melt their edges.

If your neighborhood is covered with grass, concrete, or some other surface that isn't good for tracking, you can still study tracks. Doctor James Halfpenny, a leading animal sign expert, offers some suggestions. Try sprinkling flour on the ground. Then put a dab of peanut butter in the center of the flour. The next morning, look for tracks in the flour made by animals looking for a snack.

For a track record that you can study for a long time, Doctor Halfpenny suggests putting the peanut butter at one end of a board. Put an inkpad at the other end. Make sure that to get to the bait, animals will have to walk across the inkpad and along the board.

In addition to identifying a track, you may want to know how long ago it was made. Doctor Halfpenny recommends making test prints with your own foot and watching how the prints change over time. Make a footprint in different surfaces such as dirt, sand, and snow. Notice that your footprint looks

To learn animal signs, you have to know what animals live in the habitat where you are studying. This tracking class in southern Arizona studies only the signs of desert animals.

bigger on soft surfaces and smaller on hard surfaces. One hour after making the first print, make another. Do the same a few hours later, and several hours after that. Make more tracks the next day, and a few days later. After you make each new print, compare it to the ones you already made. Note how changes in the weather affect the condition of your prints.

When you find a track and want to know how long ago it was made, step down next to it. Compare the appearance of your footprint with that of the animal's track. Then think about how the different tracks in your tests changed over time. Also, think about recent weather, and how that might have affected the track's appearance. This should give you a rough idea of how old the mystery track is.

Keeping a Sign Record

Photography is a great way to keep a record of tracks and other signs. Film with a speed or rating of 200 or higher will give you good pictures when it's cloudy, or when the sign is in the shade. Get as close as your camera will allow, and stand directly over or in front of the sign. Put a coin or ruler next to the sign to show its size.

You can also record tracks by making plaster of Paris casts. Plaster of Paris is available at most hardware stores. When you find a track you want to preserve, combine the plaster with water until it looks like thick pancake batter. Slowly pour the mixture into the track until it starts to overflow the track's edges. Let it harden for about fifteen minutes. For tracks in snow, gently spray on water from a spray bottle first. When the water freezes, you'll have a firm surface on which to pour the plaster of Paris.

Animals drop objects in their environment such as scat and hair. Members of the deer family drop their antlers each winter and grow new ones in the spring. This mule deer antler probably got caught in the bush while its owner was eating.

Chapter Three

Dropped Signs

You may think all animal droppings look the same. They don't. Still, naming the exact species of animal a scat sample came from can be just as hard as identifying tracks. You can usually narrow down the possibilities, though. Scat size and shape may help you identify the animal's family. Most members of the weasel family, including weasels, martens, and minks, leave long, thin scat that curves back on itself. Rabbit scat is small and round like little marbles. Tiny scat less than one-quarter inch (64 millimeters) long comes from either the mouse or squirrel families.

Within a family, large animals leave bigger scat than small animals. Jackrabbits' scat is generally bigger than the scat of their smaller relatives, the cottontail rabbits. In the deer family, elk scat is usually larger than deer scat, and moose scat is usually larger than the scat of both deer and elk. Likewise, wolf scat is usually larger than coyote scat, which is usually larger than fox scat. Exceptions are common, though. A young wolf may leave the same size droppings as those from an adult fox.

Scat that is dry and crumbly has probably been there for a long time. Moist scat isn't very old—especially if there are flies on it. However, a recent rain or snow could have moistened the scat. Warm scat is very fresh. If the scat is still steaming, look around carefully. The animal that left these droppings may be watching you.

Plant Eaters

If a scat sample contains seeds, stems, or leaves, it may have come from an ungulate or some other plant eater. The kind of plants an animal eats affects its scat. Beavers eat tree bark. If you notice a chunk of woody scat in a pond, it probably came from a beaver. Blue scat means the animal found a berry patch. Scientists who can name plants by their seeds will tell you what an animal ate by studying the seeds in its scat.

In spring and summer, ungulates graze on juicy grasses and herbs. This adds extra water to their scat. The summer

Communicating With Scat

Some animals leave scat on logs, rocks, or on top of the scat of other animals to mark their territories, or just to show they were there.

Collecting Scat

A scat collection is a good way to review what you have learned and teach others.

When you find a piece of scat, put it in a plastic bag. Place the bag in a hard container so the scat won't get crushed as you carry it. Write down where you found the sample, and note other signs nearby. At home, take the samples out of the bags to dry. You can apply a coat of varnish to help preserve them. After handling scat, don't touch your mouth or eyes, and be sure to wash your hands.

droppings of both elk and moose form "pats" or "pies" like those of domestic cattle, but smaller. Deer scat takes the form of soft, moist pellets, which may clump together during the summer.

In winter, elk, deer, and moose get most of their food by **browsing**, or nibbling on the branches of trees and bushes. This dry diet turns the scat of all three of these animals into dry, hard pellets. These pellets may be caved in on one end and pointed at the other end.

When bison eat dry plants, they drop stacks of disk-shaped scat. During the spring and summer months, bison enjoy fresh green plants, such as grass, which causes their scat to plop down as large, round "chips." Pioneers traveling west

These bison droppings are hard and layered because of the animal's dry winter diet. During the spring and summer, when bison eat green grass and other juicy plants, their scat is soft, moist, and pie-shaped.

Doggie Doo

Meat causes canine scat to be thin with pointed ends. Dog food from the store contains little meat. So domestic dog scat is thick with blunt ends.

burned dried buffalo chips in their campfires because they found few trees for firewood.

Meat Eaters

If you find scat containing hair, feathers, fish scales, or pieces of bone, it must have come from a meat-eater such as a member of the cat, dog, or weasel families. A meat eater's scat is usually long and narrow. Meat makes scat black. But if the animal took in lots of hair with its meal, its scat will be gray.

Canine scat comes out as one continuous piece, and gets pinched off into a narrow point as it leaves the animal's body. Feline scat is less pointy and may be divided into sections. Cat family members often scratch their front feet on the ground to bury their scat. Scratch marks and covered scat are common feline signs.

Cats often scrape the ground to cover their scat. This scraping was made recently by a house cat.

A meat eater's scat may contain some plant material. Canines and felines sometimes include grass and other plants in their diet. In Alaska, bear scat often contains both fish bones and berry seeds, because bears eat lots of berries and salmon. If a meat eater eats an animal's stomach, and the stomach contains plants, the plants will show up in the meat eater's scat.

Bird Signs

The tracks of many birds show three toes. Some species show a fourth toe sticking out the back. A small number have four toes arranged in an 'X.' Sparrows, jays, and other birds that usually perch in trees hop with their feet together. Their tracks are paired. Birds that spend lots of time on the ground such as ducks, geese, pheasants, and ravens generally walk instead of hop. They have an alternate track pattern.

A white substance, often called "whitewash," usually covers part of a bird's scat. A streak of whitewash is a good marker of where a bird has been (top photo). Owls, hawks, and certain other birds throw up some waste as rounded **pellets**. Pellets look like scat, but they contain only feathers, fur, and bones, with none of the mud-like material found in scat (bottom photo).

Feathers are common bird signs. A feather pile may mark where a predator ate a bird.

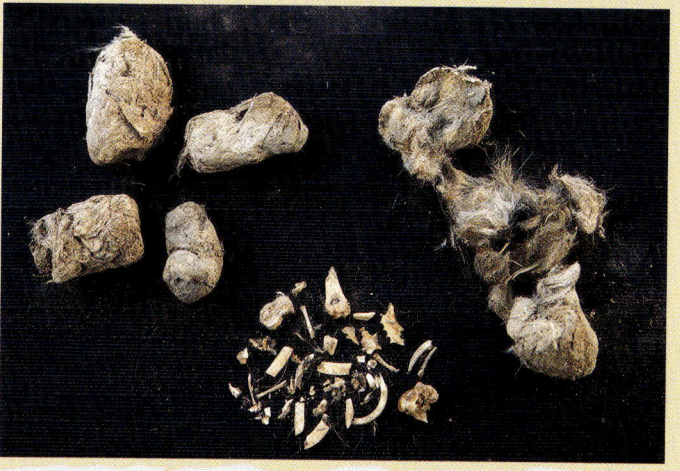

The easiest way to identify what bird made a nest is to wait for the nest's owner to return. Make sure you're far enough away so you don't scare the bird. This bird is a great egret.

Chapter Four

Among the Trees

Trees provide lots of places for animals to live and find food. However, a mature forest may have so many plants that finding tracks can be difficult, unless it snows. Some forest signs don't last long. A spider web may blow apart in the wind. The slimy trail left by a crawling slug may glisten in the sun during the morning, but disappear by midday. Leaves chewed on by caterpillars fall to the ground and rot away. However, nests made of sticks or mud may take a long time to fall apart. Also, many forest animals rub, climb, and chew on the trees, leaving signs that last for years.

Rub Marks and Scratch Marks

Bears like to rub their backs against trees. This breaks off the lower branches. Bears also scratch the bark with their claws, or tear off the outer bark to get at the sweet inner bark. Sometimes a hungry bear will tear open a dead tree to raid a beehive for honey.

When a bear climbs a tree it may leave claw marks in the bark. At least one expert thinks bears scratch their claws on trees to communicate with other bears.

Deer, moose, and elk mark small trees with the bony, branching structures on top of their heads called **antlers**. Antlers fall off in the winter and grow back during the spring and summer. A fuzzy skin called **velvet** covers the growing antlers and supplies them with food, water, and oxygen. In late summer and fall, when their antlers are fully grown, the animals rub the velvet off against young trees. The rubbing removes tree bark to form a sign called an **antler rub.**

Either elk or mule deer made these antler rubs on young aspen trees. Sometimes an animal rubs its antlers so hard that the tree bends over and breaks.

Mule deer ate all the lower needles on these conifer trees to create a browse line.

Chew Marks

How can you tell an antler rub from a place where animals have scraped the tree with their teeth? Most antler rubs have rough edges. An animal's teeth, though, usually make tree scars with clean edges. However, when deer and their relatives scrape tree bark with their front teeth, the top edge of the scrape may be rough. That's because deer have no upper front teeth to bite the bark off.

When deer and elk browse on branches during the winter, a **browse line** may form at the highest point they can reach. Below the browse line, most of the smaller branch ends have been nibbled away.

Most of the small animals that chew or gnaw on trees, branches, and twigs are **rodents**. In fact, the word *rodent* comes from the Latin word "to gnaw." Mice, rats, squirrels, beavers, and porcupines are all rodents. As an animal gnaws on trees and branches, its teeth leave grooves in the wood. Mice gnaw tiny grooves close to the ground. Beavers and porcupines make larger grooves one-eighth inch (32 mm) to one-quarter inch (64 mm) wide that are over one foot (30.5 centimeters) above the ground.

In general, large animals chew areas that are larger and higher above the ground than small animals. Some chew marks are so high that you can tell that the animal must have climbed the tree. These marks were probably the work of a porcupine or a tree squirrel. Deep snow can serve as a platform for small animals to chew higher on trees than they otherwise would.

Safe Homes

Trees provide safe homes for many different kinds of animals. Tree squirrels make nests out of grass, leaves, twigs, and bark on branches next to the tree's trunk. The nests are slightly larger than a basketball, and look like blobs of plant material. A squirrel enters and leaves its hollow nest through an opening in the side.

Bird nests may be the most common animal signs you will see among the trees. It's hard for enemies to reach a bird's eggs or chicks when they are safe in a high tree nest. Birds build

Bark for Dinner
The inner bark of trees has lots of sugar and starch. It can keep animals from starving during the winter.

More Squirrel Signs
As squirrels eat the seeds inside the cones of pines and other trees, they drop the cone scales. Some squirrels always eat at the same spot, leaving large scale piles called **middens**.

You will probably see galls more often than you'll see the insects that made them. The main gall-producing insects are gall wasps, gall midges, and gall aphids or lice. A gall's size, color, and shape can often be used to identify the insect species.

their nests from many different kinds of materials, depending on their species. They may use sticks, leaves, grass, mud, bark strips, hair, spider web silk, bits of trash, the shed skins of snakes, or a combination of materials. Most nests are built on top of the branches of trees and shrubs, or woven into places where branches fork. Some bird nests hang from tree branches. You can find bird nests by following a bird carrying nesting material. Or, if you come across some broken eggshells, look up. The nest may be above you.

Many other creatures find safety inside trees and other plants. Pine bark beetles eat their way beneath tree bark, where they cut twisting tunnels to lay their eggs. When the eggs hatch, the young beetles, called **larva**, make the tunnels

bigger. You can see the bark beetle tunnels after the tree dies and the bark falls away.

There are other insects that bite their way into branches, twigs, leaves, buds, flowers, and roots to lay their eggs. After the eggs hatch, the plants swell around the larva. The swellings, called **galls**, provide the insects living inside with food and protection. Insects cause many different kinds of galls in North America. Certain worms and microscopic life forms can cause galls too.

A pile of sawdust at the base of a tree may signal the work of carpenter ants. These insects create complex tunnel networks inside wood that protect the ant colony while they raise their young. Carpenter ants also dig into logs, fence posts, telephone poles, and buildings. Unlike termites, which also tunnel though wood, carpenter ants do not eat the wood. They only live in it.

Some hornets and wasps chew wood into fine pieces that they turn into a papery substance. They use the "paper" to

The network of beetle tunnels on the inner surface of this bark looks like a work of art.

Tent caterpillars hatch in the spring. After they hatch and build a silky nest such as the one shown here, they crawl along tree branches to eat the leaves. Look for the white trails of silk they leave on the branches. These trails lead their nest mates to the food.

enclose their hanging nests. Take a close look at the nests during the winter, when the stinging insects are gone.

Mud dauber wasps build nests of mud on trees, rocks, bridges, and buildings. The wasps kill insects or spiders and place them in the nests. Then they lay eggs on their victims.

Later, after the eggs hatch, the victims serve as the young wasps' food.

Sometimes, you can follow much of an insect's life cycle by watching for signs. Many insects attach egg cases to plants and other objects. The eggs of some insects hatch into larvae that look very different from the adult insect. Tent caterpillars, the larvae of one kind of reddish-colored moth, build silky tent-like nests in trees. All the tent caterpillars hatched from a single egg case help to build one nest in which they live between trips to eat the tree's leaves.

A caterpillar or other insect larva eventually changes into a **pupa**. The pupa of a butterfly or moth is also called a **chrysalis**. A pupa can't move or eat. It just stays in one place, and gradually changes into an adult insect. During this change, a capsule called a **cocoon** surrounds and protects the pupa. You can sometimes find insect cocoons attached to plants, or tucked into the cracks of logs or bark.

Grass arches over a rabbit runway.

Chapter Five

In the Open

Grasses and other plants usually cover open ground that isn't shaded by trees. Areas of thick grass are not good places to look for tracks. Grass blades spring back up after being stepped on, so no tracks are left behind. Grassy areas aren't a complete loss, though. Rabbits often take the same routes between their hiding and feeding places day after day. Runways form along these routes. Sometimes, grasses arch over the runways to form tunnels. Rabbits also scrape out bare spots, called **forms**, under bushes. Here they hide and stay cool during the heat of the day.

Rabbits' Feet

Rabbits and hares have long hind prints and small front prints. Their toes don't show in their tracks because the bottoms of their feet are covered by hair.

Grass leaves and stems that look like they were cut may be the bite signs of hungry animals. Grazing animals sometimes leave trails by nibbling on plants along their paths. Torn cobwebs are another sign that an animal walked through the grass.

On the grasslands in the middle of North America, grasses cover some very old signs surrounding large boulders. Long ago, bison rubbed their itchy hides against the boulders' rough surfaces. As the years passed, thousands of bison hoofs cut trenches into the earth around these natural scratching posts.

Many thousands of bison must have scratched their itchy hides against this boulder to wear a trench into the soil beside it. Today, there are no bison on the piece of prairie where the boulder sits, and the trench is covered with grasses.

Going Underground

Deserts are drier than grasslands, but these areas do have some things in common. Because both environments have few trees, there aren't as many places for animals to hide as there are in forests. That's one reason why many desert and grassland creatures dig underground homes called **burrows**. Burrows are also good places to escape summer's heat and winter's cold.

In America's southwestern deserts you can often tell what type of animal lives in a burrow by the size of the entrance hole. Small ground squirrels dig burrow holes that are 1.5 to 2.5 inches (3.8 to 6.4 cm) across. The burrow holes of larger squirrels and kangaroo rats are 3 to 5 inches (7.6 to 12.7 cm). Skunk burrow holes measure 5 to 7 inches (12.7 to 17.8 cm), while kit fox and badger holes are 7 to 12 inches (17.8 to 30.5 cm). A burrow hole over 12 inches (30.5 cm) wide is the home of a coyote.

To decide on the exact species that made a burrow hole, you may have to use other clues, such as tracks or habitat. For example, three species of pocket mice live in the same general area. Each makes a burrow hole that is 1 to 1.5 inches wide (2.5 to 3.8 cm), but each species lives in a different habitat. The Arizona pocket mouse lives in sandy open areas with bushes. The desert pocket mouse prefers sandy areas along stream beds. Rock pocket mice live in rocky areas.

On America's western plains, prairie dogs are the most visible rodents. The prairie dog is a type of ground squirrel. As a prairie dog digs its burrow, it throws dirt out the entrance

The prairie dog uses the mound at its burrow entrance as a lookout post for danger.

hole. The dirt may pile up one or two feet around the hole to form a mound that looks like a little volcano.

The animal that lives in a burrow may not be the animal that made it. Coyotes enlarge the burrows of other animals such as badgers. Burrowing owls often use the unoccupied holes of other animals. So do snakes.

Ants are some of the most familiar underground animals. Mounds of dirt or "ant hills" may be small mounds of dirt piled up around a tunnel entrance. Or they may be a foot or more high and contain a network of tunnels.

Desert Signs

Sandy desert soil is an excellent place to see the curving tracks of a snake. If the curves are big, the snake was moving fast. A slow-moving snake leaves small curves, or a line that is nearly straight, as if someone dragged a stick along the ground.

Cactuses are abundant desert plants. A cactus's thick body is covered with pointy spines instead of leaves. Birds called cactus wrens, thrashers, and roadrunners build nests amid the long spines of the cholla cactus. The cholla's sharp spines keep snakes from reaching the nest and eating the baby birds.

The gila woodpecker's home is the giant saguaro cactus. This robin-sized bird pounds its nest holes into the saguaro's sides. The curving wall of the nest dries out and becomes hard. After the cactus dies, the soft parts rot away. However, the

Tail Draggers

Long-tailed animals leave lines with their footprints when they drag their tails. Kangaroo rats and many lizards are common desert tail draggers.

There can be no doubt about the curving track of a snake such as this prairie rattler.

The hole in this saguaro cactus leads to a gila woodpecker nest cavity like the one this person found in an old saguaro skeleton.

boot-shaped nest wall lies on the ground for many years amid the saguaro's wooden skeleton.

Some desert animals actually eat cactus, spines and all. The javelina, or peccary, a relative of the pig, munches on the prickly pear cactus. It bites out big, rounded sections from the prickly pear pads.

Packrats, also known as desert woodrats, build large nests of twigs and other materials against cactuses, trees, bushes, or the backs of shallow caves. They are the junk collectors of the animal kingdom. Aluminum cans, old shoes, tin foil, car parts, and toys are just some of the items that people have found in packrat nests. A packrat may coat part of its nest with its

A packrat leaves chew marks on a juicy desert plant.

droppings. It urinates on the scat, which then becomes black and gooey like tar. The urine helps to preserve the scat. Because packrats often use the same nest as their ancestors, some of the nests and their sticky coatings may be hundreds of years old.

In the High Country

Winters on the highest mountains are too cold for trees, but the high country is home to a variety of plants and animals. The mountain goat is one of the most beautiful high country creatures. This ungulate's shaggy white coat keeps it warm during the winter. By late spring, the mountain weather warms up, and the mountain goat no longer needs such a thick

Words of Caution

When exploring the desert, be careful of thorns, spines, and rattlesnakes, and carry plenty of water.

A mountain goat scratches itself on a bush, leaving behind clumps of hair.

coat. Its hair falls away in chunks, and gets snagged in the bushes. American Indians living in the Northwest collected mountain goat hair to make blankets.

The mountain goat spends much of its time on the steepest, rockiest slopes where it is safe from enemies. The two toes of its cloven foot spread apart for balancing on narrow ledges and pointy rocks. This causes the mountain goat's tracks to look somewhat square, rather than heart-shaped like deer tracks. Bighorn sheep, the mountain goat's high country neighbors, have similar square-shaped tracks.

Small mountain creatures, such as the pika (a relative of the rabbit), hide from the mountain winters. All summer long, pikas gather plants. A pile of plants drying on a rock is a sure sign of a pika in the neighborhood. The pika stores the dry plants in its den beneath the rocks as a winter food source.

The pocket gopher is another small mountain animal that hides from the winter weather. In summer, it pushes dirt out of its underground tunnels to form cone-shaped mounds. During the winter, it digs tunnels in both the snow and the ground. Sometimes it moves loose dirt from its underground tunnels into its snow tunnels. As the snow melts, the dirt settles out as long ribbons of soil called **castings**.

Each summer, as mountain snows melt, dirt castings from the inside of pocket gopher snow tunnels settle to the ground.

The rising sun shines on the dips and piles of sand formed by a sea turtle's flippers as it crawled from the sea to lay its eggs during the night.

Chapter Six

Along the Shore

Land next to water is full of life. Many animals leave their tracks in the sand and mud at edges of streams, rivers, lakes, ponds, and oceans. Some come to eat. Others come to drink. Still other animals, such as sea turtles, reproduce along the shore.

A shoreline stroll may turn up the web-footed prints of gulls, ducks, geese, or swans. The webbing connects their toes and helps them swim. Marks from the webbing may not show up on a hard surface. So if you find a large, three-toed bird track near the water, look around for some webbed tracks too. The beaver's rear foot is also webbed. However, beavers have five toes.

Builders and Diggers

No animal leaves more noticeable signs than the beaver. Beavers are swimming creatures that need deep water to escape enemies. If a shallow stream is the only water in a beaver's neighborhood, the beaver dams the stream to make a pond. First, it cuts down trees using its teeth. Then it hauls tree branches and logs down to the water as dam-building materials. You can recognize a beaver pond by the dam, by the many tree stumps around the pond, and by dead trees killed by the rising water. Also, twigs and branches with their bark removed, and lying near fresh water, are the remains of a beaver's meal.

If you find a beaver dam, look around for other signs, such as stumps, fallen trees, and the beaver's lodge. You may also find drag marks where the beaver hauled logs and limbs to the water, and wood chips marking a spot where the beaver worked.

Another sign of a beaver pond is the beaver's **lodge**, or house, standing in the water. A beaver lodge may be more than five feet high by fifteen feet around. It is made of the same kind of woody materials as the dam. A pair of beaver parents lives with their young inside this hollow, dome-shaped mass. They enter and leave through underwater openings.

The muskrat, another water-loving animal, also builds a mound-shaped house in shallow water. Grasses, water plants, and sticks are their main building materials.

Some crayfish are builders too. Many of these relatives of shrimp and lobsters burrow into the edges of streams, lakes, and ponds just below the waterline. There are other crayfish, however, that burrow in the moist soil near the water. As they dig, they place lumps of mud around the entrance holes, to form little chimneys.

Mud chimneys mark the entrances to crayfish burrows in this Louisiana field.

Bank Beaver

Beavers living along deep water don't make dams and lodges. They burrow into the bank of the river or lake.

49

The purple sea urchin, which lives in the shallow water along America's West Coast, makes a hole too—in solid rock. By moving the jaws on its underside and the spines covering its body, the urchin slowly wears the rock away. As the animal grows, its hole gets deeper. However, the mouth of the hole stays the same size as when the urchin was small. In time, the urchin becomes trapped within its rocky cave.

Birds called bank swallows and northern rough-winged swallows are two more shoreline diggers. They dig burrows in steep riverbank cliffs. Their cousins, the cliff swallows, build ball-shaped nests of mud on cliffs and under bridges.

Blue-footed boobies and certain other sea birds build their nests on islands where they are safe from egg-eating enemies. However, the nests themselves offer little protection. The boobie's nest is nothing but a few sticks and feathers on the ground.

Many ocean animals living in the water near shore build containers for their eggs. The moon snail cements sand grains together to form a ring-shaped egg cover. You may find one of these **sand collars**, as they are called,

This scrape in the ground may not look like a nest, but it's all the blue-footed boobie needs.

washed up on the beach. You may also find the chains of beige-colored egg chambers laid by another sea snail, called the whelk. The black rectangular egg case of a relative of the shark, called a skate, may also get washed in with the waves. Each corner of a skate egg case curls out into a long, thin horn.

Ancient Signs

A hundred million years ago, dinosaurs stomped through the mud beside an ancient ocean. Later, more mud, plus sand, covered the dinosaurs' giant tracks. Millions of years passed. The soft sand and mud turned to rock. Eventually, streams washed away the rock that hid the tracks.

Today, you can see dinosaur footprints in Texas, Colorado, and other places. The tracks tell scientists what species of dinosaurs lived in these areas. The scientists can also figure out how fast the dinosaurs walked by measuring the distance between the tracks.

Like all animals, the dinosaurs left no written records. Still, you can tell they were here from the signs they left behind. You may also be able to figure out what they did, if you know what to look for.

The dinosaur that made these tracks was an Acrocanthosaurus, *a 20- to 30-foot long relative of* Tyrannosaurus Rex. *The tracks are 1 to 2 feet long and a foot or more wide.*

Glossary

alternate track pattern—one footprint appears in front of the corresponding footprint on the opposite side of the animal

antler—a branching, bony structure projecting from the head of an animal in the deer family

antler rub—bark removed from a tree where a member of the deer family rubbed velvet off its antlers

browse line—the highest point browsing deer can reach and below which the branch ends have all been chewed off

browsing—eating the ends of branches on trees and bushes

burrow—a hole or tunnel in the earth dug by an animal, or the act of digging such a hole or tunnel

canine—refers to the dog family or a member of the dog family

castings—cores of earth from pocket gopher snow tunnels left on the ground after the snow melts

chrysalis—the pupa of a butterfly or moth

cloven foot—the hoof of certain ungulates which is divided into two parts, each part being a modified toe

cocoon—an envelope that an insect forms around itself and in which it passes the pupa stage

dewclaw—a small toe that serves no practical use

family—a group of different species with similar characteristics

feline—refers to the cat family or a member of the cat family

form—a spot of bare ground scraped by a rabbit or other animal under plants as a place to hide and rest

gall—a swelling in a plant caused by an insect, worm, or microscopic life form

habitat—the special surroundings preferred by an animal for its survival

hibernate—to pass the winter in a state of deep rest or sleep

hoof—a hard, bony covering on an ungulate's toe made of the same substance as a claw or nail in other animals

larva—an early stage in the life of some animals such as insects

lodge—the home of sticks and logs a beaver makes in its pond

midden—a large pile of cone scales dropped by a tree squirrel eating the seeds in the cones

pad—a soft thickening on the underside of an animal's foot

paired track pattern—two footprints on opposite sides of an animal's body appear side by side

pellet—a small rounded mass of waste containing feathers, fur, or bones thrown up by certain birds

pupa—a stage in the life of certain insects between the larva and the adult

rodent—a small gnawing animal

sand collar—a collar-shaped structure of sand, made by the moon snail for depositing its eggs

scat—droppings of solid animal waste

sign—any marking, object, or structure an animal leaves in its environment. Some people refer to tracks in a separate category from other signs such as droppings, chew marks, nests, diggings, etc.

species—a group of animals that can mate and reproduce healthy young

spoor—a word of Dutch origin referring to animal sign

track—a footprint or other imprint made on a surface

tracking—following a line of prints or other signs that make up an animal's trail

track pattern—the arrangement of tracks in relation to each other

trail—a line of tracks or other sign

ungulate—an animal that eats plants, often has some kind of horns or antlers, and usually has hoofs covering its toes

velvet—the fuzzy skin that covers and supplies growing antlers with food, water, and oxygen

To Find Out More

Books

Arnosky, Jim. *Crinkleroots Book of Animal Tracking*. New York: Bradbury Press, 1989.

Dorros, Arthur. *Animal Tracks*. New York: Scholastic, 1991.

Kudlinski, Kathleen V. *Animal Tracks and Traces*. Danbury, CT: Franklin Watts, 1991.

Mason, George F. *Animal Tracks*. Hamden, CT: Linnet Books, 1988.

Nail, James D. *Whose Tracks Are These?* Niwot, CO: Roberts Rinehart, 1994.

Selsam, Millicent E. and Joyce Hunt. *A First Look at Bird Nests*. New York: Walker and Company, 1984.

Organizations and Online Sites

Boy Scouts of America
1325 West Walnut Hill Lane
Irving, TX 75015-2079
http://www.geocities.com/~pack215/wildlife.html
The Boy Scouts website, "Tracking and Stalking North American Wildlife," provides information about tracking in general, and about the biology and tracks of individual species.

The Tracker, Inc.
P.O. Box 173
Asbury, NJ 08802
http://www.trackerschool.com
This school is run by Tom Brown, Jr., one of America's leading animal sign experts. The website provides an "Animal Tracking for Kids" link, and the school's Coyote Tracks Program offers courses for kids and teens.

Keeping Trak
P.O. Box 848
Richmond, VT 05477
e-mail: keeptrak@together.net
Offers youth programs, and also visits schools to provide children with the knowledge they need to monitor wildlife in their area.

National Audubon Society
700 Broadway, 5th floor
New York, New York 10003
http://www.audubon.org
Some local Audubon chapters offer programs about wildlife and tracking. The national office can put you in touch with a local chapter near you.

National Wildlife Federation
8925 Leesburg Pike
Vienna, VA 22184
http://www.nwf.org/
Their "Animal Tracks" program teaches about wildlife, tracking, and other environmental subjects.

A Note on Sources

Years ago I read a book by Olaus J. Murie called *A Field Guide to Animal Tracks*. I also read Tom Brown's autobiographical account of tracking and wildlife study titled *The Tracker*. Those books made me want to learn more. Since then, whenever I see an article about animal signs in a magazine or newspaper, I tear it out or make a photocopy for my files. When I walk in a forest, desert, or some other natural area, I keep a lookout for tracks, scat, and other signs. One of my favorite activities, wildlife photography, puts me in close touch with animals and their signs. These things helped prepare me to write this book. I also consulted the following: *A Field Guide to the Mammals* by William Henry Burt and Richard Phillip Grossenheider, *Exploring Nature in Winter* by Alan M. Cvancara and Daniel F. Richards, *Familiar Animal Tracks* by John Farrand, Jr., *A Field Guide to Mammal Tracking in North America* by James Halfpenny and Elizabeth Biesiot, *The*

Complete Tracker by Len McDougall, and *Tracking and the Art of Seeing* by Paul Rezendes. Most of these books are enriched with the authors' personal stories about wild animals and their signs.

— Frank Staub

Index

Numbers in *italics* indicate illustrations.

Alternate track patterns, 16, 25
Antler rubs, 29, *29*
Antlers, *20*, 29

Bank swallows, 50
Bark, 31–33
Bark beetles, 32–33
Beaver lodges, *48*, 49
Beavers, 48–49
Beetle tunnels, 32–33, *33*
Beetles, *10*, 32–33
Birds, *26*, 35, 41
   scat, 25
   tracks, 25
Blue-footed boobies, 50, *50*
Browse lines, 30, *30*
Browsing, 23
Burrows, 39–40, *40*, 49, *49*

Cactuses, 41, *42*
Canines
   scat, 24–25
   tracks, 12–13, *12*
Carpenter ants, 33
Castings, 45, *45*
Caterpillars, 35
Chew marks, 31–32
Cholla cactus, 41
Chrysalis, 35
Cloven feet, 14, 44
Cocoons, 35
Communication
   with scat, 22
   with scratch marks, *28*
Crayfish, 49

Dauber wasps, 34–35
Desert woodrats. *See* packrats.
Deserts, 39, 40–43
Dewclaws, 14

61

Dinosaur tracks, 51, *51*
Droppings. *See* scat.

Egg chambers, 51. *See also* nests.

Families, 14–15
Feathers, 25
Feline
   scat, 24–25, *24*
   tracks, 12
Footprints. *See* tracks.
Forest signs, 27
Forms, 37

Galls, 32, 33
Gila woodpeckers, 41–42
Grasslands, 37–38

Habitats, 14
Halfpenny, James, 17
Heels, 12
Hibernation, 15
Hooves, 13–14, *13*
Hornets, 33–34

Injuries, 8, *9*
Insects, 32–35

Larva, 32

Middens, 31
Mountain goats, 43–45
Mountain regions, 43–44
Muskrats, 49

Nests, *26*, 27–28, 31–32, 34, *34*, 42, 50, *50*. *See also* egg chambers.
Northern rough-winged swallows, 50

Packrats, 42–43, *43*
Pads, 13
Paired track patterns, 16, *16*, 25
Pellets, 25
Photography, 19
Pikas, 45
Plant-eating animals. *See* ungulates.
Pocket gophers, 45
Prairie dogs, 39–40, *40*
Prickly pear cactus, 42
Pupa, 35

Rabbits, 37
   scat, 21
   tracks, 38
Rodents, 31
Rub marks, 28–29

Runways, *36*, 37

Saguaro cactus, 41–42, *42*
Sand collars, 50–51
Scat, 8, 21–22, *23*
   animal identification with, 21–22
   bird, 25
   canine, 24–25
   collecting, 23
   communication with, 22
   diet and, 22–23
   feline, 24–25, *24*
   shape of, 21–23
   size of, 21–22
   usage of, 23–24, 42–43
Scratch marks, 24, *24*, 28–29, *28*, *29*, 38, *38*, *44*
Sea urchins, 50
Shorelines, *46*, 47, 50
Signs, 27
Skates, 51
Snake tracks, 41, *41*
Spoors, 8
Squirrel tracks, 15
Swallows, 50

Tail draggers, 41
Tent caterpillars, 35
Tracking, 11, 16–17, *18*

Tracks, *6*, 7–8, *10*, 11, *13*, 15, *46*
   birds, 25
   canine, 12–13, *12*
   dinosaur, 51, *51*
   feline, 12
   heels, 12
   hooves, 13, *13*
   mountain goats, 44–45
   pads, 13
   patterns, 15–16, *16*, 25
   rabbit, 38
   recording, 18–19
   snake, 41, *41*
   surface conditions and, 17
   tail dragging, 41
   weather and, 19
   web-footed prints, 47–48
Trails, 11, 15

Ungulates, 13–14, 22, 43

Velvet, 29

Wasps, 33–34
Weather, 19
Web-footed prints, 47–48
Whelk, 51
"Whitewash," 25
Wounds. *See* injuries.

About the Author

Frank Staub is a photographer and writer. His photographs have been featured in twenty-eight books, many of which he also wrote. He has covered subjects ranging from manatees to mountain goats and from Yucatan to Yellowstone. His photographs have appeared in dozens of other publications, and he has authored numerous magazine articles and audiovisual productions. He has worked as a whitewater river guide, truck driver, railroad track laborer, veterinary assistant, and high school science teacher. He holds an undergraduate degree in biology from Muhlenberg College, and a master's degree in zoology from the University of Rhode Island. He currently lives in Tucson, Arizona and spends his free time bicycling, hiking, diving, and climbing mountains. This is his first book for the Watts Library.

Best Cats & Kittens

Billy Grinslott & Kinsey Marie Books
ISBN - 9781960612809

Persian cats are considered one of the earliest pedigreed breeds, with the first purebred Persian cat arriving in the United States around 1875. Persian cats were showcased in the world's first organized cat show in 1871. Persian cats come in different colors. Famous for their long, thick fur, Persian cats are quite the high-maintenance breed, with combing and de-shedding needed daily.

The American shorthair breed crossed the ocean with European pioneers on the Mayflower to America in 1620. They were used to control the mice population on the ship while traveling to America. American shorthairs don't need a lot of attention to be happy. Because of this, they are a great choice of cat for a single person who works all day. They are relaxed, calm, and gentle with children. Also, they tend to be quiet and well-behaved.

Himalayan Cats have brilliant blue eyes. They have cream-colored bodies with a darker face, ears, feet, and tail. They are a longer haired cat and need extra grooming. Himalayan cats love to cuddle, be petted, and spend time interacting with their family. These cats enjoy playing with toys. They have a great bond with their owners.

The British Shorthair cat grows up to be a fairly large cat. When fully grown, they are not the kind of pet you will easily pick up when you want to cuddle, and they will eat adequate amounts of cat food. They are one of the oldest cat breeds. British Shorthair cats are slow to mature, and this applies to both their physical and mental attributes. British Shorthair cats are known for having kind, loving natures, being laid back, and showing loyalty to their owners.

Curious and clown-like, the Cornish Rex cat thrives on entertaining people. This cat has kitten-like energy well into adulthood. They like to play and love to be picked up and handled or cuddled with. Their short coat is ideal because of low shedding and minimal grooming. Their fur comes in more than 40 different colors and patterns.

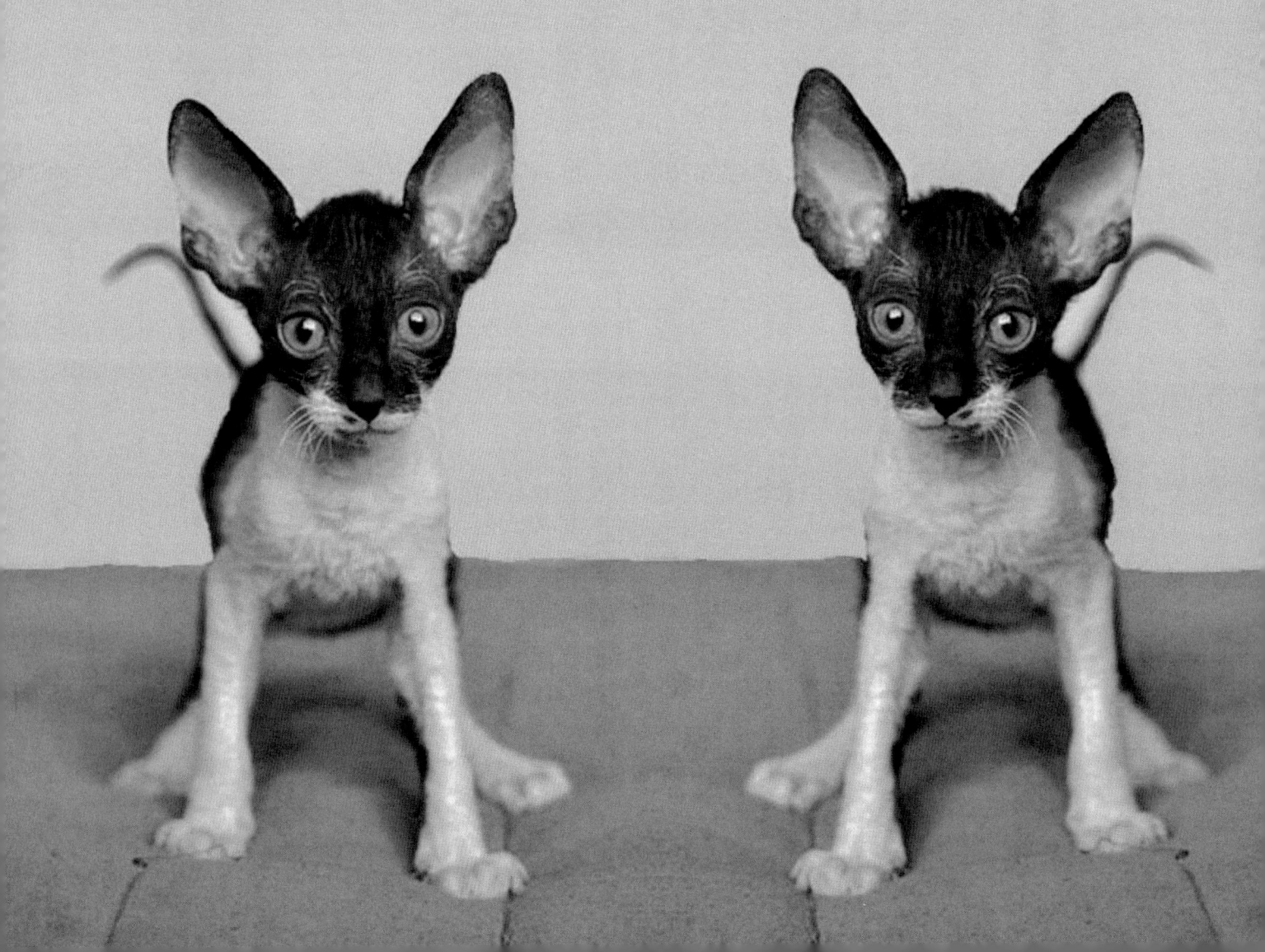

Devon Rex cats are known for being curious, playful, and mischievous. It should come as little surprise that these cats enjoy jumping up to the highest point in a room or on your shoulder. The Devon cat is happiest when they are around others. They are social animals and do not always enjoy being left home alone, especially for a long time. Devon Rex cats are intelligent. They can learn many of the same tricks and commands people typically teach dogs.

The Scottish Fold got its name because its ears lay flat. They are born with straight ears. The fold begins to develop when the kitten is between 18 and 24 days old, but only if they have the gene that is responsible for the fold. Scottish folds are known for their sweet personalities and fun quirks. Oftentimes, they will sit up like people to improve their vantage point when they hear a noise. One downfall is their tail does not flex like other cats. You will have to be careful when handling them so you don't hurt their tail.

A Bengal cats coat features spots, rosettes, and marbling, giving them an exotic, jungle cat appearance. In fact, the Bengal is the only domestic cat breed with rosette markings. These cats are highly active and almost always on the move. Bengal cats love to play with people and will vocalize their desire to interact with you. Bengal cats love to play in the water. It's not unusual for a Bengal cat to join his owner in the shower.

Ragamuffin kittens are born white and develop a different color pattern as they mature. These gentle giants are one of the largest cat breeds. These cats are known for having two different colored eyes. Ragamuffins are docile, friendly and have a sweet temperament. They love companionship. Their pleasant demeanor makes them excellent pets for homes with children and other animals. These cats are attention-seekers, who enjoy playtime, walks on a leash, and can even learn a trick or two.

Siberian cats have a thick long coat. It's a triple coat, which means that the cats grow three layers of fur. This evolved to help them adapt to harsh cold Siberian winters. Gentle, adaptable, and incredibly smart, the Siberian is a fun cat to be around. But they can have vastly different personalities. Siberian cats are super social animals who adore their owners and generally don't like being left alone too long. These cats are best fit for a home where people are usually around and willing to engage in play.

Manx cats have long back legs and can jump extraordinarily high. They can jump 4 feet high from a standing position. Their long back legs also make them extremely fast runners. One other feature you will notice is they have no tail or a very short tail. They typically have an arched back. They come in a variety of different colors. Many Manx cats suffer from a variety of painful symptoms that are collectively referred to as Manx Syndrome, including spina bifida.

Bombay cats are easily recognized by their shiny, black coats, feet, and nose. These cats are habitual heat-seekers. It's not uncommon to find a Bombay cat resting peacefully near any heat source. They love to curl up on a sunny window ledge, or on top of their owner. The Bombay's short hair doesn't require much grooming. Bombay cats tend to keep close to their owners. They will seek their owner's attention and have been known to follow their favorite person from room to room.

The Japanese Bobtail cat has a short tail. Their tail is more like a rabbit's tail than that of other cats. The tails on these cats are all unique, and no two are alike. They can also have two different colored eyes. The Japanese Bobtail is an active, sweet, loving and intelligent cat. They love to be with people and will play endlessly. They learn their name and respond to it. They bring toys to people and play fetch with a favorite toy for hours.

Burmese cats are incredibly trusting with limited survival instincts, which makes them an easy target for predators if left outdoors. Its better to keep them indoors. They aren't shy about vocalizing their needs. When they need your attention, they'll let you know with a raspy, guttural rumble. These frisky cats have a humorous side. They are intelligent cats who can learn to play fetch and enjoy interactive toys and puzzle feeders.

The Norwegian Forest cat has a thick double-layered coat which keeps them warm in cold climates. It also repels water which makes them waterproof. The Norwegian Forest Cat makes a great family pet. They are affectionate and form strong bonds with all family members.

The Maine coon cat is the largest domesticated cat. A Maine Coon is in the record books as the longest domestic cat in the world, measuring over four feet long. Not to worry, these big cats are very gentle and like to be around people. They are very playful and can be walked on a leash. They also make a chirping sound, instead of a meow. They also like water and taking baths, which most cats don't.

Birman kittens are born all white, their colors begin appearing when they are a few weeks old. Birman cats are a quiet breed. They are not overly talkative, and they could make a great pet for someone who prefers to have a quiet home. These cats are known to be curious, and they can sometimes find themselves in sticky situations. They are easy-going and have a kind demeanor. A great choice for families with children or other cats or dogs.

Sphynx cats don't look like cats, and they resemble moles. Sphynx might be hairless cats, but they are full of love and affection. Owners will tell you that Sphynx cats have a friendly nature. They love their owners and generally get along with dogs and other cats. If you are looking for a loving cat companion, they make an excellent choice. This cat can get cold quickly since they have no fur to protect them from cold. It's better to keep them indoors.

The Tiffany is also known as the Chantilly cat. This cat breed is relatively rare in the United States, so it's not always easy finding one. Tiffanies will hold a conversation with you or make a chirping sound when they want your attention. This cat is fluffy, friendly, fun loving and loves to roll over. They also trill, chirp, and like to do tricks.

The Ragdoll was given its name because of the cat's tendency to go limp when lifted, just like a rag doll. They are one of the largest breeds of domestic cats. When Ragdolls are born, they are pure white and develop their coat color and pattern over the first 2 weeks of their life. They love to play and sometimes enjoy a game of fetch. They are often known as puppy-like as they follow people around and they are very loyal. Just like dogs, a Ragdoll cat will often greet you when you come home.

the Abyssinian is not a lethargic lap cat. These highly active cats are always on the move. Their athleticism and curiosity result in a breed that is constantly jumping, climbing, and exploring. The Abyssinian has cougar-like appearance, thanks to its ticked coat. It's a coat has individual strands that alternate bands of color. Abys love to interact with people. They have a dog-like attachment to their owners and prefer to be an involved member of the family.

Ocicats are among the breeds of cats who enjoy water and may try to join you in the shower or bathtub. This cat won't turn down an invitation to ride in cars or travel with you. They are incredibly athletic and can jump to high spots, balance on narrow ledges, and get to places other cats probably wouldn't think of. This cat enjoys a lot of attention and very able to demand it when they need it.

Somali cats have a bushy tail and large ears and has the nickname of Fox Cat. These cats are slow to grow, and they won't reach full maturity until 18 months of age. The Somali is an active cat who loves to jump and play. They are an easy cat to have in your home. Somalis love people and other animals. These cats are not aggressive, but they are persistent in getting what they want. Once something triggers curiosity. Their desire for satisfy their curious mind, these clever cats won't be shy about snooping in your cabinets and finding themselves some mischief.

Exotics Shorthairs are sometimes born with long hair. Exotics Shorthairs are not jumpers or sprinters, although they still like to run around in the house. The Exotic Shorthair is as low maintenance and laid back. This kitty has a double layer coat, with a thick, downy under layer that lifts the topcoat away from the body. With their adorable, teddy bear appearance, the Exotic Shorthair is regularly featured in movies. They are the second most popular cat in the US. They make an all around good pet in many ways.

Chartreux cats enjoy being lap cats and curling up near you whenever you are relaxing on the couch. These cats are relatively quiet. Not only do they not talk often, but even when they do, they are still soft spoken. These cats do well when left alone at home, but they don't mind the extra company of another cat or dog. When it comes to caring for a Chartreux cat, everything is standard, these cats can be a great choice for first-time cat parents. Chartreux are relatively easy to please, but do like to play on a daily basis.

Tonkinese cats can jump to great heights, but don't worry, these cats are not known to be mischievous. Although they appear to be a lean medium sized cat, you will be surprised by their weight when you pick one up. They are a muscular cat which makes them weigh more. This cat loves to be outdoors. If kept indoors make sure you have things around the house like toys and scratching posts. These cats like spending time with people, they do not do well with being left alone for hours. Having other pets around helps to keep them from getting bored.

The American Bobtail cat has a stubby tail like a bobcat. American Bobtails are fascinated by shiny objects. This means that you should be careful of where you leave your jewelry or loose change, they may take it. These cats are like Houdini the magician. They have been known to escape from closed rooms and open doors. These cats are outgoing, empathetic, and they make for excellent companions. They are playful, friendly, and intelligent. They like spending time with their family, and they get along with dogs, and other cats.

Siamese kittens are born a creamy white color. Their darker color patterns develop later. Most cats are known for their sharp acute vision, especially at night. But Siamese cats have a genetic flaw that makes it difficult for them to see color and distinguish details at night. Their eyes will look crossed because of this. Siamese cats are social, they are very friendly. They are a great cuddly companion. They are great for families with dogs and small children.

The Selkirk Rex is an interesting cat breed, easily recognized by their long curly coat. These cats developed their curls through a natural genetic mutation. Everything about this cat is curly, even its whiskers. The Selkirk rex is the only breed of cat named for a real person. Some Selkirk's get dirty easily, so it's recommended to keep up with routine baths to keep them clean. A Selkirk is active, yet still affectionate, and does well in a home with children as well as other pets.

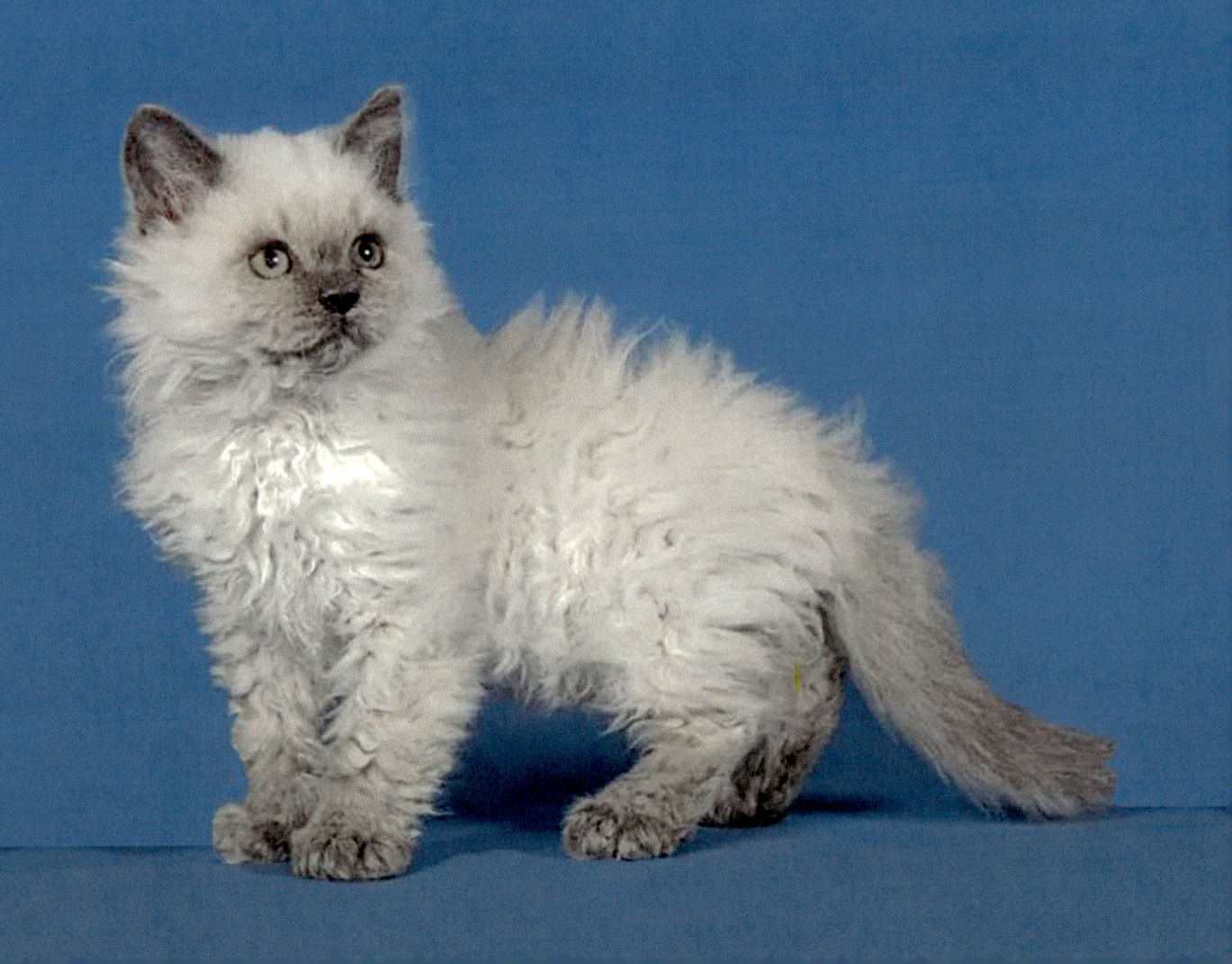

The oriental shorthair has unusual looks. The Oriental Shorthair is thought to be one of the most intelligent cats, if not the most intelligent. They are highly trainable because they are very curious, and they love interaction and stimulation. They get attached to people, very quickly. Oriental Shorthairs are ready to bond with their family. it's not unusual for an Oriental shorthair to live more than 15 years. Oriental Shorthair breed is known for its honking sounds, a few cats only make this sound when feeling frustrated or upset

The American Curl cat got its name because its ears curl. American curl cats are born with straight ears. They begin to curl in three to five days' time, and they settle into their fully curled shape within about four months. They are nicknamed the Peter Pan of cats because of their playful, kitten like personalities. It's important to always handle American curl ears with care, to not damage their ear cartilage.

The Toyger cat got its name because it has tiger like stripes. Toyger cats have shorter legs than other breeds, which is a common trait of big cats. They also have long toes and big paws like big cats. They have a positive personality, such as a pleasant temperament, relaxed personality, intelligence, trainability, and ease of handling. They are content to live with people, including children. They make good pets.

Author Page

Billy Grinslott & Kinsey Marie Books

Copyright, All Rights Reserved

ISBN - 9781960612809

Made in the USA
Middletown, DE
17 March 2024